Lingo Dingo
and the
Dutch chef

Written by Mark Pallis
Illustrated by James Cottell

For my awesome sons Oscar and Felix - MP

For Leo and Juniper - JC

LINGO DINGO AND THE DUTCH CHEF

Story edited by Natascha Biebow, Blue Elephant Storyshaping
First Printing, 2022
ISBN: 978-1-915337-25-2
markpallis.com

Lingo Dingo
and the
Dutch chef

Written by Mark Pallis

Illustrated by James Cottell

NEU WESTEND
— PRESS —

This is Lingo. She's a Dingo and she loves helping.
Anyone. Anytime. Anyhow.

Lingo often helps her stylish neighbour Gunther, who lives by himself next door. She does a few jobs and has a nice chat. It makes Gunter feel good and it makes Lingo feel good too.

One day, Lingo arranged a special birthday party for Gunther. She even ordered a cake from a famous Dutch chef.

There was a knock at the door, "It must be the cake!" said Lingo.
But it was a monkey.

"Hallo. Mijn naam is Chef Nono.
Ik heb een probleem," he said.

Oh no. I can't speak Dutch yet, thought
Lingo. *Maybe 'hallo' is like 'hello'.*

hallo = hello; **mijn naam is** = my name is;
ik heb een probleem = I have a problem

"Hallo," said Lingo. Chef Nono replied slowly,
"Het spijt me. Ik kan de verjaardagstaart niet maken."

"I don't understand," said Lingo. "But let me guess. You want…"

het spijt me = I am sorry; **verjaardagstaart** = birthday cake;
Ik kan de verjaardagstaart niet maken = I cannot make the birthday cake

een **karretje** = a trolley; een **augurk** = a gherkin;
ballonnen = balloons; **nee** = no

"Mijn oven is stuk," explained Chef Nono.
"Kan ik jouw oven gebruiken?"

Chef's oven must be broken thought Lingo. "I know!
Let's bake the cake together," she said.

mijn oven = my oven; **is stuk** = is broken;
kan ik = can I; **Kan ik jouw oven gebruiken?** = can I use your oven?

Chef tapped his wrist. "Hoe laat is het? Negen uur? Tien uur?" he asked.

Lingo showed Chef her watch.

"Elf uur? Laten we beginnen! Snel!" They only had one hour until the party.

hoe laat is het? = what time is it?; **negen uur** = nine o'clock; **tien uur** = ten o'clock; **Elf uur** = eleven o'clock; **laten we beginnen** = let's go; **snel** = quick

Chef Nono and Lingo whizzed around the kitchen:

Een schort voor jou.

Een garde.

Een mengkom.

een schort = an apron; **voor jou** = for you; **een garde** = a whisk;
een mengkom = a mixing bowl

"Geef me de boter, suiker, eieren en bloem, alsjeblieft," said Chef.

Lingo wasn't sure what those words meant, so she just grabbed fish, coffee and onions instead.

"Vis, koffie, en uien. Walgelijk!" laughed Chef.

Geef me, , = pass me; **boter** = butter; **suiker** = sugar; **eieren** = eggs; **en** = and; **bloem** = flour; **alsjeblieft** = please; **vis** = fish; **koffie** = coffee; **uien** = onions; **walgelijk** = gross

Chef plopped butter, sugar, eggs and flour into a bowl. "So that's what 'boter, suiker, eieren en bloem' means!" laughed Lingo.

"Ik meng, jij mengt, wij mengen," said Chef and together they began to mix the cake.

Ik meng = I mix; **jij mengt** = you mix; **wij mengen** = we mix

"Ten slotte bakpoeder. Twee lepels vol," said Chef. Lingo guessed 'bakpoeder' meant baking powder, but how much?

Before she could ask, Chef hurried away, saying, "Excuseer me. Ik moet een plasje doen."

Lingo laughed, "I can guess what 'ik moet een plasje doen' means!"

ten slotte = finally; bakpoeder = baking powder; twee = two;
lepels vol = spoonfulls; excuseer me = excuse me; ik moet een plasje doen = I need to do a wee wee

I wonder if this is too much? thought Lingo as she added ten spoonfulls of 'bakpoeder' to the mix.

She carefully put everything into the oven and before long, a sweet cakey smell filled the kitchen.

bakpoeder = baking powder

"Wat is er gebeurd? Het is enorm!" said Chef.

Lingo realised she had added too much baking powder.
"Sorry," she said sheepishly.

wat is er gebeurd? = what happened? **het is enorm** = it is huge

They somehow got the cake out of the oven but ...

it was so big ...

... they couldn't hold it. "Disaster!" cried Lingo. "Een ramp!" wailed Chef.

Een ramp = a disaster

"I know what will make you feel better," said Lingo, kindly. "Eat this 'augurk.'"

"Walgelijk. Ik haat augurken," said Chef.

They were running out of time.

augurk = gherkin; **walgelijk** = disgusting; **ik haat** = I hate; **augurken** = gherkins

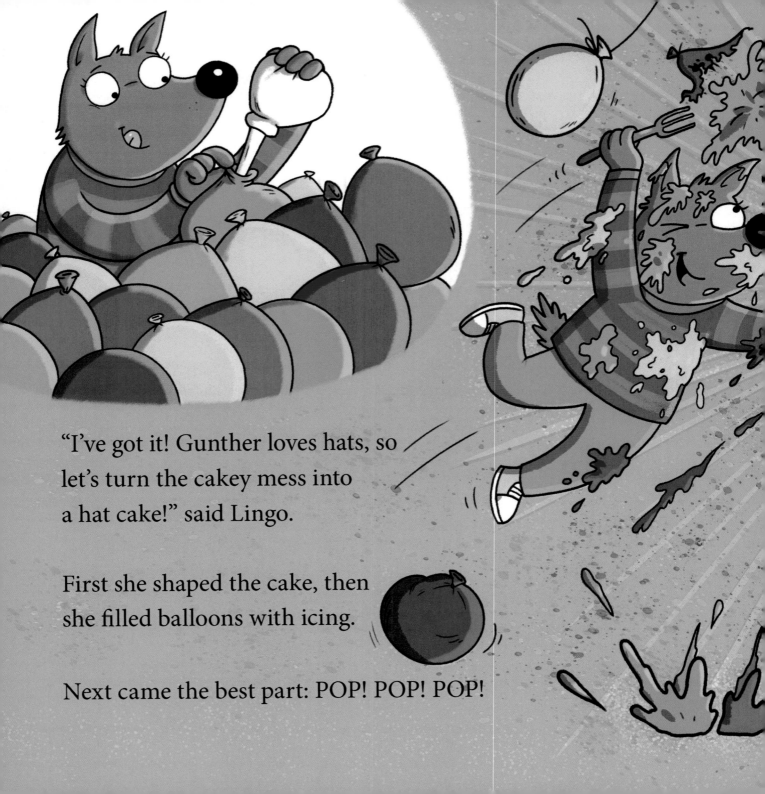

"I've got it! Gunther loves hats, so let's turn the cakey mess into a hat cake!" said Lingo.

First she shaped the cake, then she filled balloons with icing.

Next came the best part: POP! POP! POP!

It was a messy job but in the end, the cake looked fantastic.
"Rood, oranje, geel, groen, blauw. Fantastisch!" said Chef.

rood = red; **oranje** = orange; **geel** = yellow; **groen** = green; **blauw** = blue; **fantastisch** = fantastic

There was a knock at the door.
"De deur!" said Chef.
It was Gunther, and he was
wearing his special hat!

"Thank you. This makes me
feel so special," said Gunther.
"You are special," replied Lingo.

de deur = the door

Gunter was thrilled with his cake.

Chef's deep voice sang "Lang zal hij leven…"

Lang zal hij leven = Long may he live ('happy birthday to you' song)

"Blaas!" said Chef.

Gunther blew out all the candles in one puff and everyone tucked in.

blaas = blow

"Ik eet, jij eet, hij eet, zij eet, zij eten," laughed Chef.
"Wij eten," added Lingo proudly.

ik eet = I eat; jij eet = you eat; hij eet = he eats; zij eet = she eats; zij eten = they eat; wij eten = we eat

The friends watched the sun go down.

"Ik ben gelukkig,
jij bent gelukkig,
we zijn allemaal gelukkig!" cheered Chef.

ik ben gelukkig = I am happy; **jij bent gelukkig** = you are happy; **we zijn allemaal gelukkig** = we are all happ

Baking a cake, helping a friend,
learning a new language... what a day!

But now it was time for bed. It was time to dream
about all the fun things that might happen tomorrow.

Learning to love languages

An additional language opens a child's mind, broadens their horizons and enriches their emotional life. Research has shown that the time between a child's birth and their sixth or seventh birthday is a "golden period" when they are most receptive to new languages. This is because they have an in-built ability to distinguish the sounds they hear and make sense of them. The Story-powered Language Learning Method taps into these natural abilities.

How the story-powered language learning method works

We create an emotionally engaging and funny story for children and adults to enjoy together, just like any other picture book. Studies show that social interaction, like enjoying a book together, is critical in language learning.

Through the story, we introduce a relatable character who speaks only in the new language. This helps build empathy and a positive attitude towards people who speak different languages. These are both important aspects in laying the foundations for lasting language acquisition in a child's life.

As the story progresses, the child naturally works with the characters to discover the meanings of a wide range of fun new words. Strategic use of humour ensures that this subconscious learning is rewarded with laughter; the child feels good and the first seeds of a lifelong love of languages are sown.

For more information and free learning resources visit www.markpallis.com

You can learn more words and phrases with these hilarious, heartwarming stories from NEU WESTEND — PRESS —

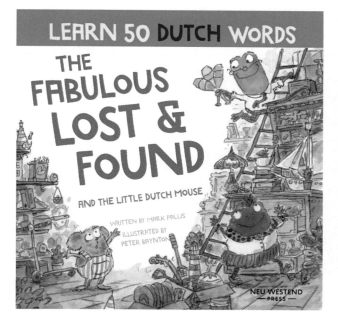

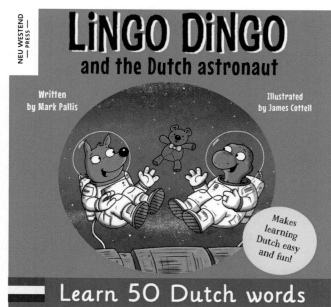

@MARK_PALLIS on twitter
www.markpallis.com

To download your FREE certifcate, and more cool stuff, visit
www.markpallis.com

@jamescottell on INSTAGRAM
www.jamescottellstudios.co.uk

> "I want people to be so busy laughing, they don't realise they're learning!"
>
> Mark Pallis

Crab and Whale is the bestselling story of how a little Crab helps a big Whale. It's carefully designed to help even the most energetic children find a moment of calm and focus. It also includes a special mindful breathing exercise and affirmation for children. Featured as one of Mindful.org's 'Seven Mindful Children's books'

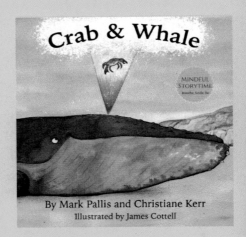

Do you call them hugs or cuddles?

In this funny, heartwarming story, you will laugh out loud as two loveable gibbons try to figure out if a hug is better than a cuddle and, in the process, learn how to get along.

A perfect story for anyone who loves a hug (or a cuddle!)

www.markpallis.com